earth & life WHY?

WHY DO ELEPHANTS HAVE BIG EARS?

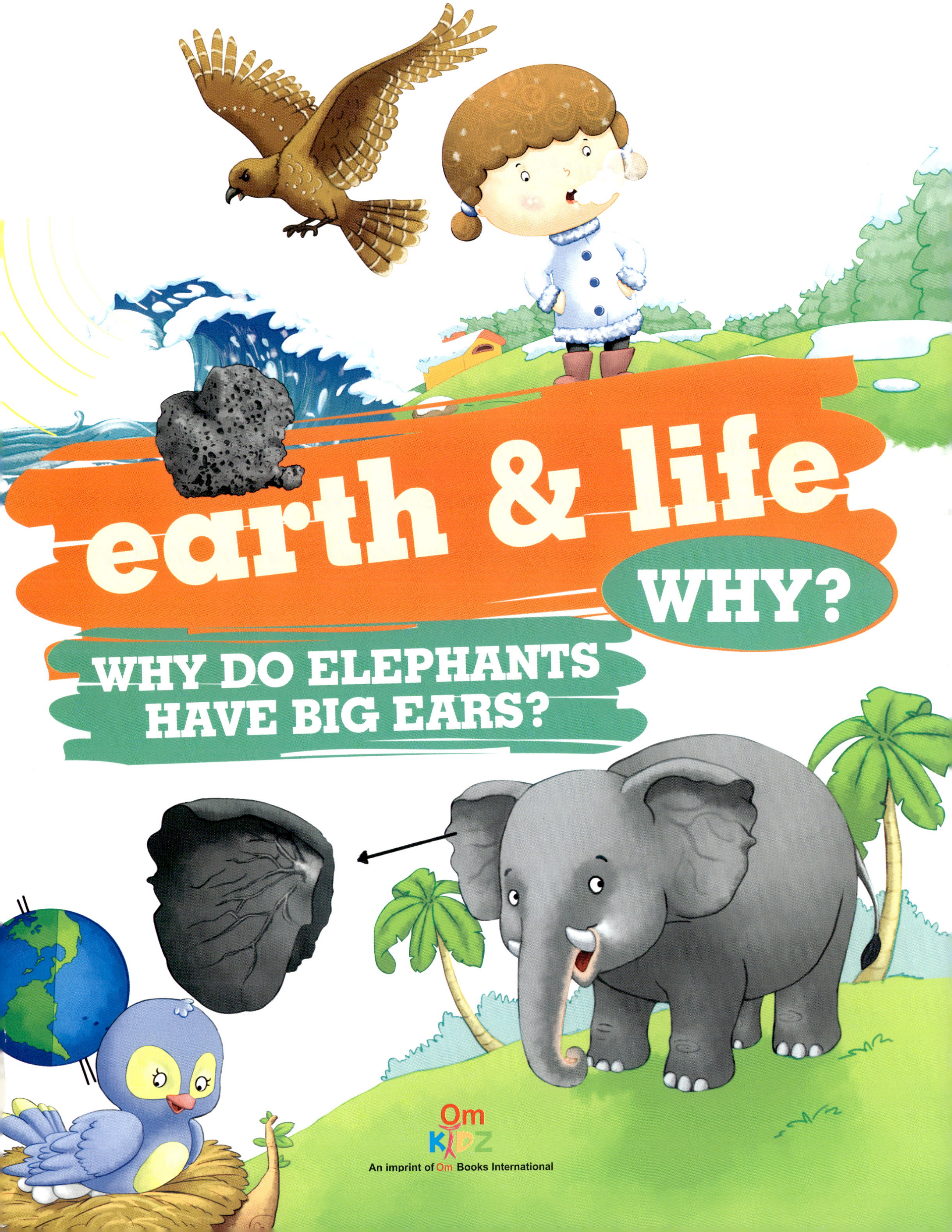

Om KIDZ
An imprint of Om Books International

WHY?

CONTENTS

WHY?

Find out!

Why doesn't bamboo need fertilisers and pesticides for growing?

1 Why is the lady's slipper flower called so?

This flower looks like a slipper, hence the name! The lady's slipper orchid is a rare and impressive orchid found in Britain. It has claret petals that frame a beautiful, bright yellow pouch which resembles a lady's slipper. Each stem of the plant has only one or two flowers.The plant's leaves have nerves along their length and are green in colour.

Pocket fact

The Rhizoctonia, a soil fungus, helps the pink and white lady's slipper plant's seeds to germinate and grow by nourishing the seedling for two or three years. Eventually, the plant grows big leaves that nourish it with the help of photosynthesis.

2 Why are the flowering habits of bamboo known to be amazing?

Flowers of the same species of bamboo bloom at the same time! Bamboo plants are known for their amazing flowering habits. There are many different kinds of bamboo with different flowering cycles. Only very few bamboo plants flower each year and most of them wait much longer. This is because all the bamboo plants of the same species flower at the same time, irrespective of which part of the world they are growing in!

Find out!

Kiwi fruits originally grew in China many years back. What were these fruits called then?

3 Why are kiwi fruits hairy on the outside?

The hairy outer cover of a kiwi fruits protects them! Kiwi fruits are hairy to keep insects and other animals away. When the hair sticks to the legs of insects, they tend to move away. Hair also helps the kiwi fruits retain its moisture. They collect the moisture from the atmosphere that keeps the fruit moist.

Pocket fact

The Japanese Yubari King cantaloupes are the most expensive fruit in the world. You would be surprised to know that once two melons were sold at an auction for $23,500!

4 Why does fruit change colour as it ripens?

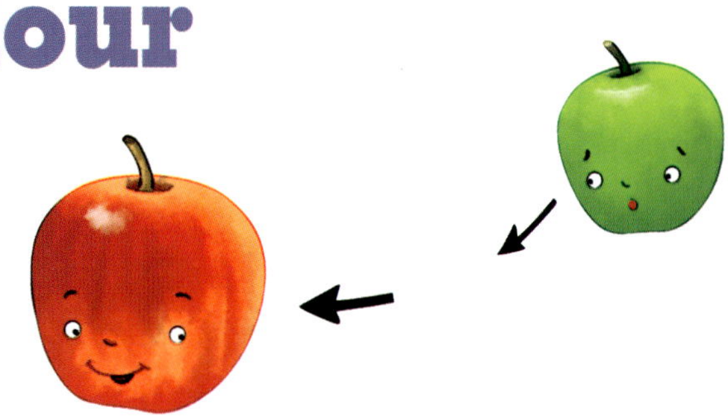

New pigments give a fruit different colours as they ripen! A fruit has a different colour when it is unripe. It ripens due to the action of the enzymes. When a fruit begins to ripen, the pigments of the fruit undergo chemical reactions and new pigments are made. This makes a fruit's skin change colour to red, yellow, brown, green, etc., making it attractive!

5 Why do some fruits have seeds?

So that we can have more plants! A seed contains a baby plant that is surrounded by a seed coat for protection. Seeds are found in fruits of flowering plants and help these plants to reproduce. But for this, seeds must be dispersed away from the parent plant before they can grow into new plants. This is done by animals (when they eat fruits), wind, water and other methods.

Pocket fact

The double coconut is the largest seed in the world. It can measure up to 50 centimetres (almost 1.6 feet!) around the middle!

6 Why doesn't a banana have seeds?

It indeed has! A banana has seeds that are immature and appear as black dots in the middle of the banana. But if you open a wild banana, you can find seeds that may be large, making the fruit hard to eat. This is why bananas have been specially bred for many years so that they are seedless triploids. A triploids has three sets of genes that do not form mature seeds.

Find out!

Why is a banana peel slippery?

Find out!

Which spice is obtained from the bark of a tree?

7 Why do trees have sap?

To carry food to different parts! Sap is a mixture of sugar, water, minerals, nutrients, and also hormones! It is an important fluid and carries food and water to different parts of the plant, and provides nourishment. Sap carries nutrients from the soil to the rest of the plant and transports food that is made in the leaves to the other parts of the plant!

8 Why does a tree have a bark?

Pocket fact

You must have enjoyed maple syrup on pancakes. The maple syrup is made from the sap of North American maple trees: sugar maple and black maple. It takes 40 gallons of maple sap to make one gallon of maple syrup!

It's a protective covering! The bark of a tree is its outermost layer of tissue, just as your skin. It helps the trees in many ways. It is like an armour for the tree and protects it from damage by different creatures. The bark protects the trees from severe heat, sunlight, cold, and is also helpful in preventing water loss from the trees!

Find out!

Why do some trees have needle-shaped leaves?

9 Why do leaves fall off trees?

To help trees survive the cold weather! Trees lose a lot of water through leaves when they make food. In winters, these trees do not get enough water to replace what they lose through the leaves. So, the trees seal the spot that connect each leaf to the branch. When this sap inside the trees cannot reach them, the leaves fall off. If a tree does not seal the spots where the leaves grow, it would die!

Pocket fact

The Ada tree of Australia has a 50-feet girth. It is 236 feet high and has a gigantic root system that spreads out to more than an acre.

10 Why are Trembling Giant Trees special?

They are a single organism in a forest! The Trembling Giant is an enormous grove of Quaking Aspen tree located in the Fishlake National Forest in Utah, US. The National Forest is made of this single organism. There are around 47,000 trees in the grove. These trees are genetically identical and all share a single root system.

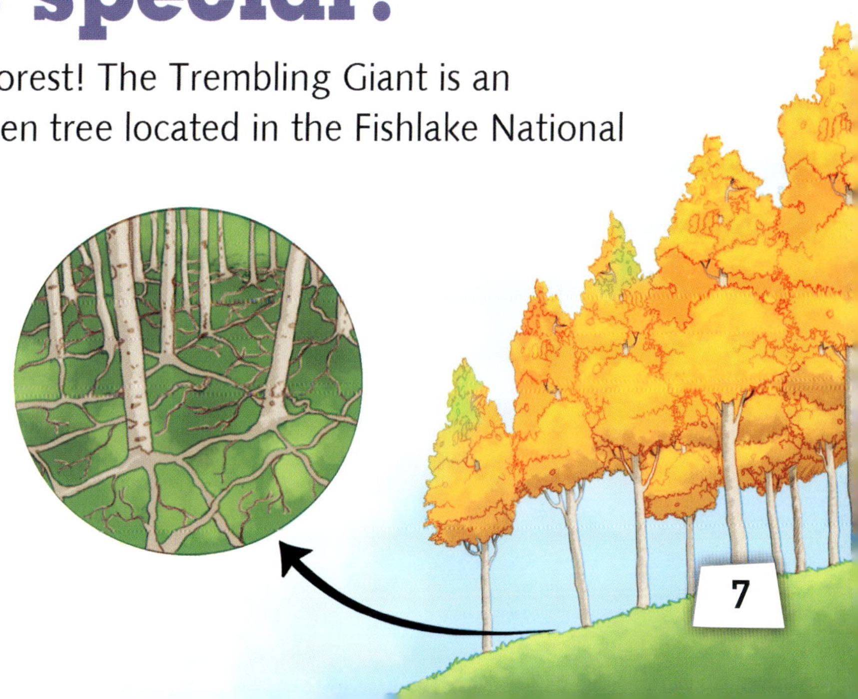

Find out!

What are the other names of potato?

11 Why do potatoes have 'eyes'?

To let new plants sprout! A potato plant does not grow from seeds, but buds. A potato has black spots that are called 'eyes'. The eye of a potato is made up of two parts: a curved scar and an axiliary bud. This bud plays an important role in the life of a potato. When you put a potato in soil and water, the axiliary buds in potato eyes sprout new plants.

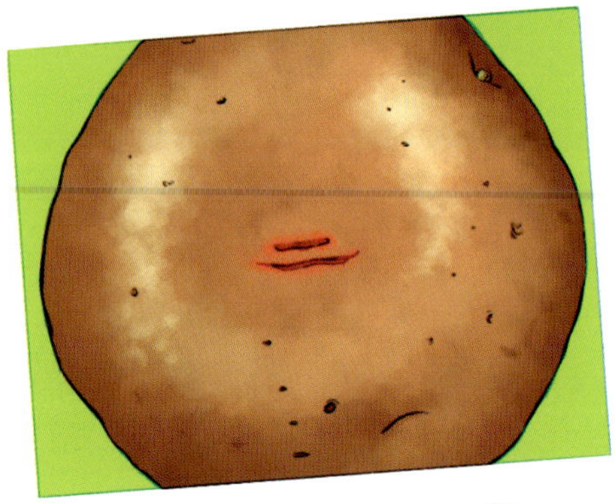

12 Why are chilli peppers spicy?

Due to some chemical compounds! The chilli pepper is actually the fruit of plants from the capsicum family. Chilli peppers have chemical compounds called capsaicinoids. These chemicals are odourless, flavourless and are hidden in the white flesh inside peppers. It is capsaicnoids that give chilli peppers their spicy flavour.

Pocket fact

Chillies originated in America. Diego Alvarez Chanca, a physician, brought chillies to Spain in 1493. He sailed with Columbus when he discovered America.

Find out!

How much water do elephants need every day?

13 Why do elephants have big ears?

Their big ears keep them cool! You sweat when you feel hot, but elephants do not sweat. They have big floppy ears to regulate their body temperature. An elephant has many tiny blood vessels on the inside of its ears close to the surface. When it is very hot outside, heat is released from the elephant's ears, keeping it cool.

Pocket fact

Giraffes only need five to thirty minutes of sleep in a day! They often take quick naps that may last only a minute or two at a time!

14 Why do giraffes have a blue-black tongue?

To protect it! A giraffe's tongue is prehensile that wraps around leaves and can grow to be 20 inches long. When a giraffe feeds, its tongue is frequently exposed to sunlight which might cause its tongue to get sunburned. This is why a giraffe's tongue has melanin: the same pigment that tans your skin when you stay out in the sun. Melanin gives a giraffe's tongue a blue black colour preventing it from being sunburned.

Find out!

Which bird lays eggs in another bird's nest?

15 Why do birds sit on their eggs?

To keep their babies warm! Birds don't give birth to young ones but lay eggs that have an embryo inside. The embryo inside the eggs cannot develop if the temperature is less than about 27°Celcius. Mother birds sit on their eggs to provide warmth so that the young ones develop properly inside the eggs. This process of providing warmth to the eggs is called incubation.

Pocket fact

The oilbird is called a 'guácharo' or 'tayo' in Spanish. It is sometimes called 'diablotin' (French for 'little devil') in Trinidad. This is because of the loud cries it makes for echolocation.

16 Why are oilbirds different from other birds?

They use echolocation just like bats! Oilbirds are the only birds that use echolocation. These birds live in caves during the day and use their rapid chirps and clicks to navigate through caves where they cannot see. Also, oilbirds are the only nocturnal fruit-eating birds in the world!

Find out!

What is an iceberg?

17 Why can I see my breath on a cold day?

Because the moisture in your breath condenses! Your breath not only contains carbon dioxide but also moisture that comes from your mouth and lungs. When you breathe out, the moisture hits the cold air. This air cannot hold much moisture. So the moisture condenses when it comes in contact with the cold air and forms a little cloud. What you see is the condensed moisture in the form of a cold breath!

Pocket fact

Yakutsk, the capital of the Republic of Yakutia in the Russian Far East, is the coldest inhabited city. Its average temperature in January is about -40° Celsius and it has been known to drop down to -64°Celsius.

18 Why doesn't the water in the ocean freeze easily?

The salt content and its movement don't let the ocean freeze easily! The salt in it lowers the freezing point. In addition to salt, ocean water also has more movement than the water in lakes and ponds. The movement of ocean water helps it retain more heat than rivers, lakes and ponds. These two factors don't let the ocean freeze easily.

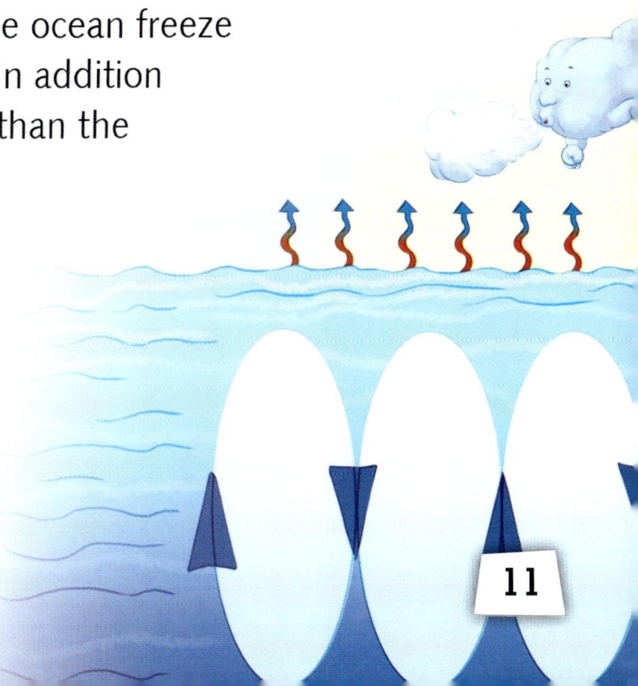

Find out!

What was the Dead Sea called many years ago?

19 Why do seas and oceans have waves?

Because of the energy passing through the water! You must have observed that the seas and oceans are never still. Waves are actually energy passing through the water, leading to its circular motion. Water gets this energy from the wind. When wind blows across the surface of the ocean, friction is caused between the wind and the water. This disturbance creates waves.

Pocket fact

Tsunamis are huge waves of water that are usually caused by earthquakes or volcanic eruptions under the sea. In December 2004, one such tsunami in the Indian Ocean off Indonesia killed over 200,000 people in 14 countries.

20 Why is the Dead Sea called the 'Dead Sea'?

Because nothing lives in it! The Dead Sea is actually a salt water lake located between Jordan and Israel. It gets its name because no plants or animals live in it. The reason for this is that the Dead Sea has six times more salt than what is present in the oceans. It also contains many dissolved minerals like magnesium chloride, calcium chloride and potassium chloride in large quantities which makes its water unfit for living organisms to survive.

Find out!

What are the objects you would find at a beach?

21 Why do some beaches have yellow sand?

Because of iron oxide! Sand is a granular material made of fine rock and mineral particles. The composition of sand varies from place to place and depends on the local rocks. The most common constituent of sand is silica, usually in the form of quartz and iron oxide. The presence of iron oxide within the quartz crystals of the sand gives it the yellow colour.

Pocket fact

Can you estimate the number of sand grains on earth? A study from the University of Hawaii states that there are approximately seven quintrillion five quadrillion grains of sand on all the beaches in the world! That is a 75 with 17 zeros, i.e, 7,500,000,000,000,000,000!

22 Why do some rocks have holes in them?

Some rocks are formed when melted rock in the form of lava or magma from a volcano cools above ground or underground. These rocks are called igneous rocks. When magma starts cooling on the surface of earth, air bubbles get trapped in it and holes are made. The air holes make these rocks lightweight. Pumice and scoria are examples of rocks with holes!

Find out!

What do mountaineers do to cope with less air on high mountains?

23 Why is it so cold in the winters?

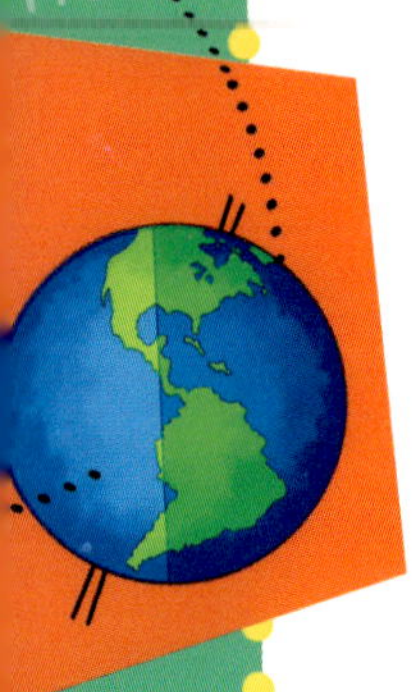

Because Earth is titled away from the Sun! The Sun heats Earth, which revolves around the Sun while rotating on its tilted axis. During the winter, Earth is tilted away from the Sun. This makes it harder for sunlight to reach the places on Earth that lie on the tilted part. Since there's less sunlight, these places become colder. The more a place is tilted away from the Sun, the chillier it gets!

Pocket fact

The coldest winter on Earth is experienced at the Polar Plateau in Antarctica. The average mean annual temperature is -58. 2° Celsius. It's chattering cold!

24 Why is it cooler up on the mountains?

Because there's less air! Sunlight reaches Earth in the form of solar radiation. This solar radiation passes through the atmosphere (layer of air that surrounds Earth) before reaching Earth's surface. Radiation is absorbed by the air and then radiated as heat. As you go higher, (on hills or mountains), the air is less dense and it doesn't absorb enough sunlight to radiate it as heat. Hence, even though mountains are closer to the Sun, they are cooler!

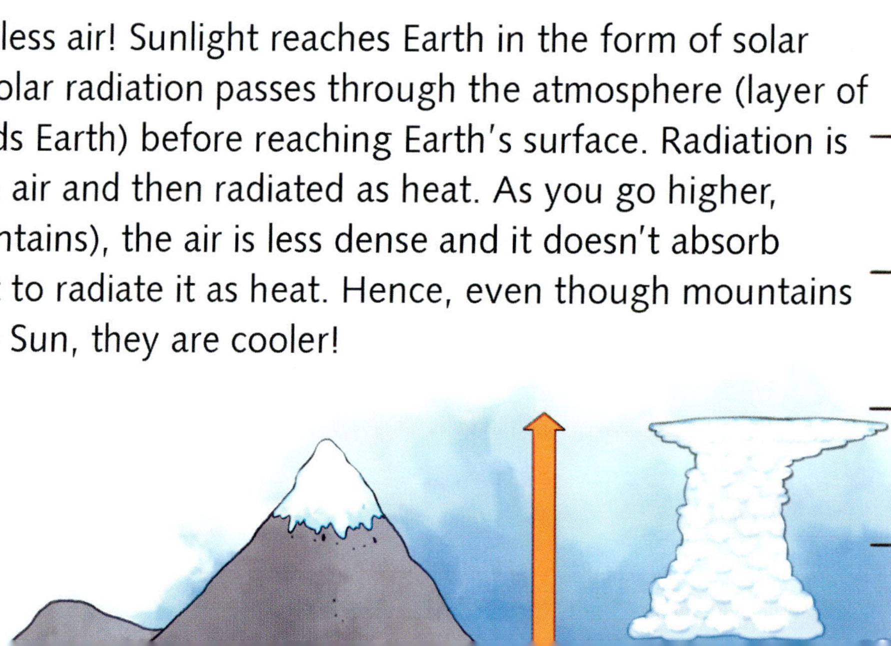

Find out!

Which is the longest river in the world? Does it experience floods?

WHY?

25 Why do rivers flood?

Have you ever tried pouring water into a glass which is already full of water? The same happens with a river when it gets extra water. It overflows and leads to a flood.

But this is a natural event that happens when the river catchment receives more than the usual amount of water through rainfall or melting snow. The river cannot cope with this extra water. This causes the level of the water in the river to rise which leads to a flood!

Pocket fact

Some algae can live in boiling hot water. These are yellow, green, and orange algae found in Yellowstone National Park, Wyoming, USA.

26 Why do some lakes turn green?

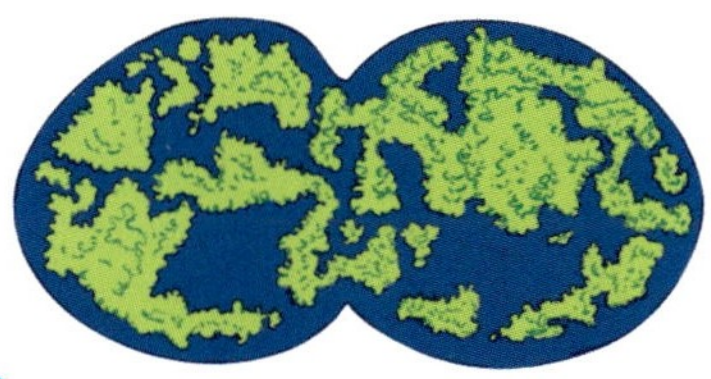

Tiny plants turn lakes green! Some lakes have tiny plants called algae. Most of them are so small that you can't even count them. These plants float on the surface of lakes to make their food using sunlight. When they multiply, they cover the surface of the lake and make the lake water appear green in colour.

OTHER TITLES IN THIS SERIES